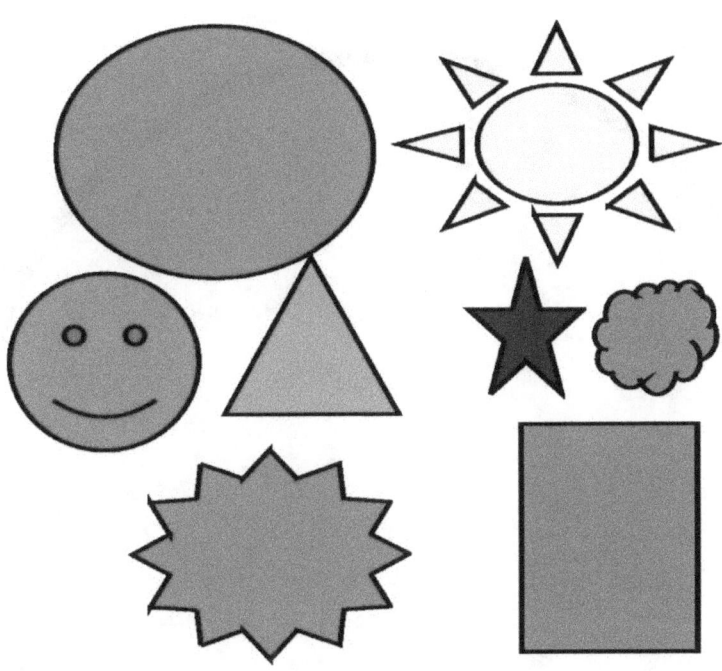

COLOURING BOOK FOR KIDS :1

SHAPES BY : SUSHMA

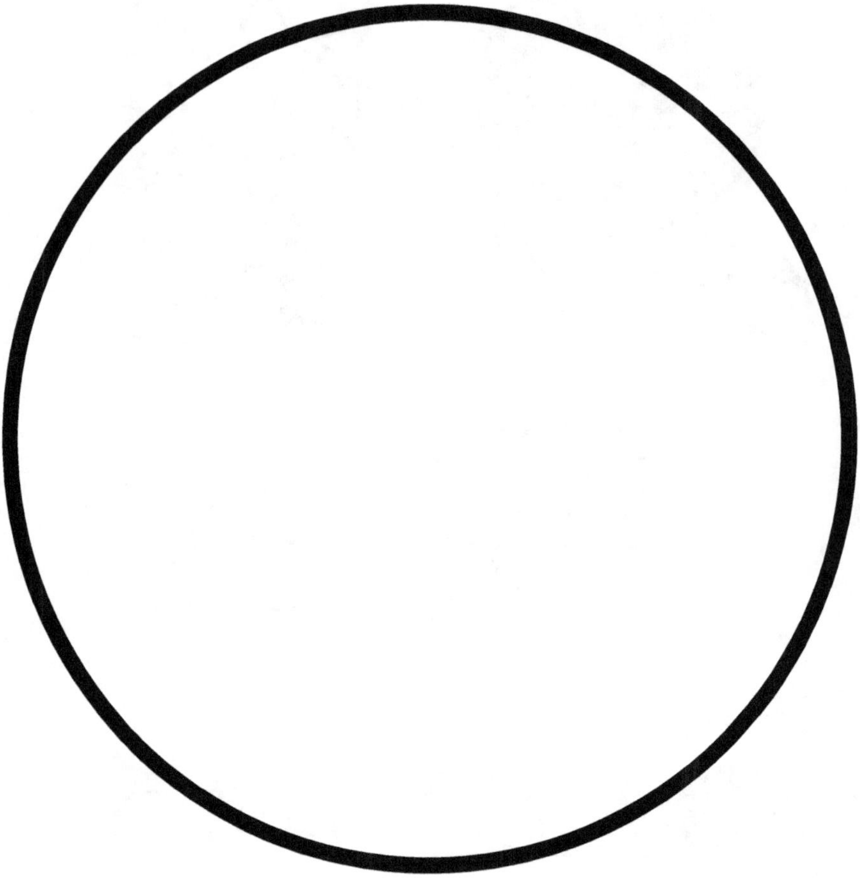

COLOURING BOOK FOR KIDS :1 SHAPES

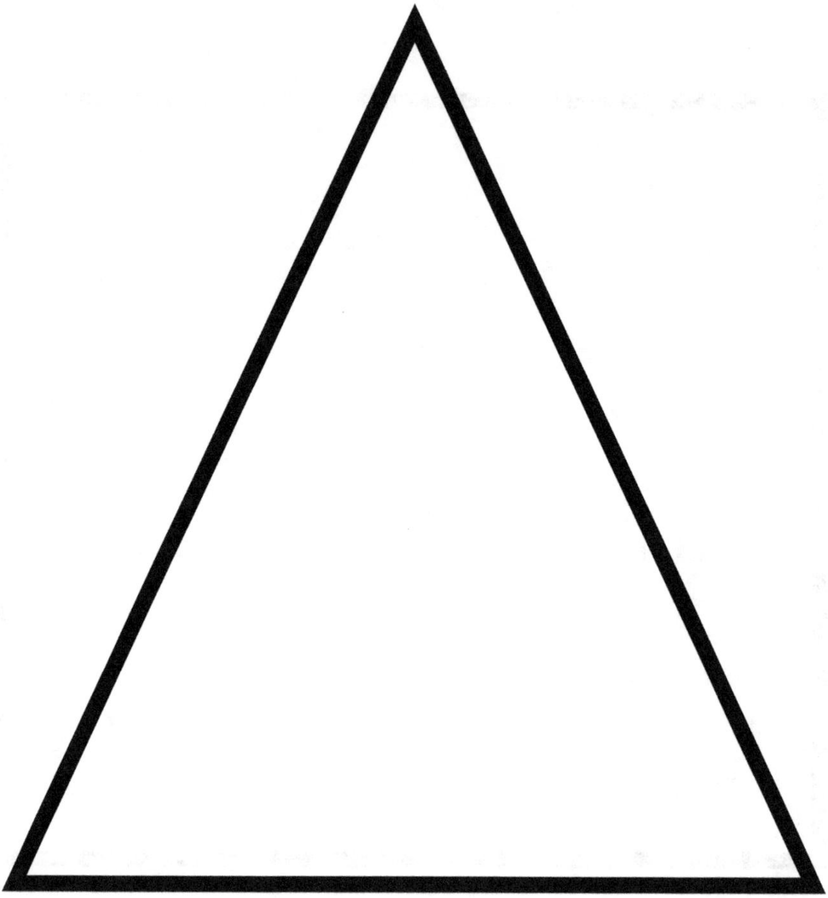

COLOURING BOOK FOR KIDS :1 SHAPES

LOURING BOOK FOR KIDS :1 SHAPES

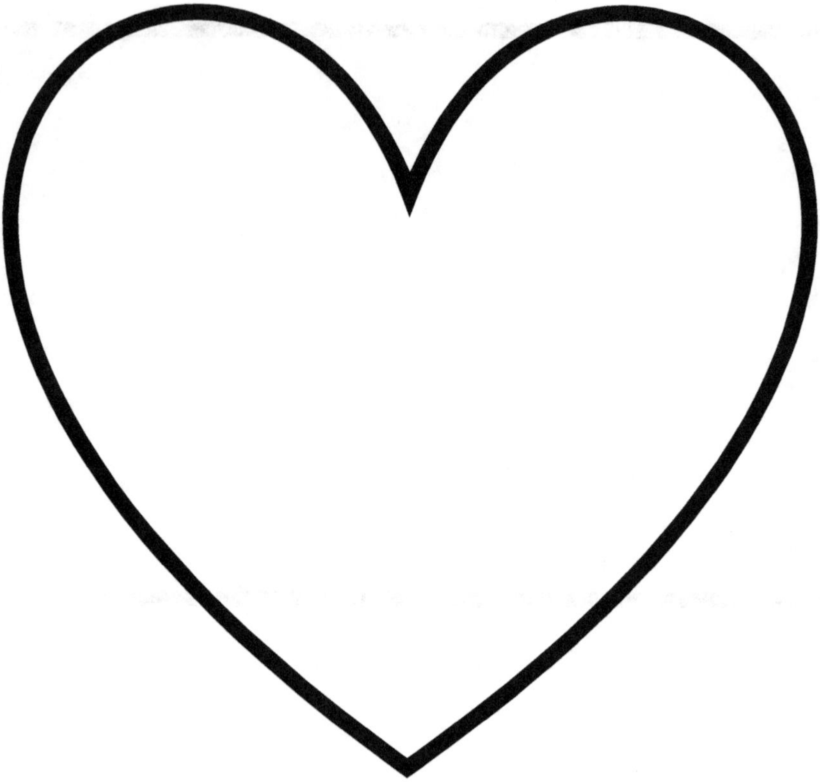

COLOURING BOOK FOR KIDS :1 SHAPES

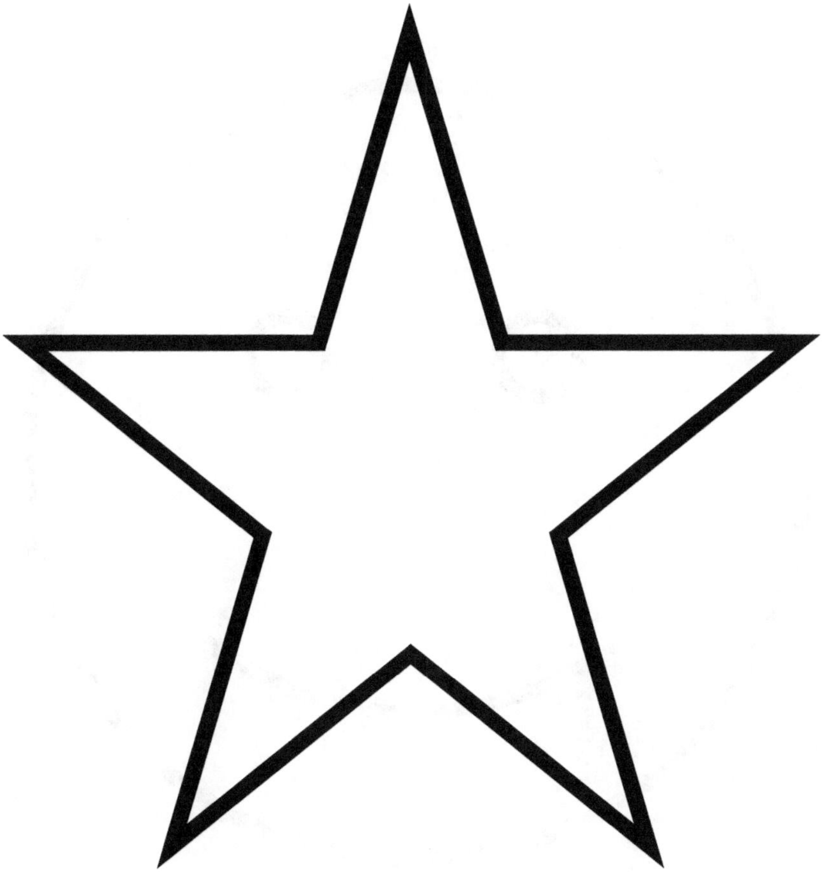

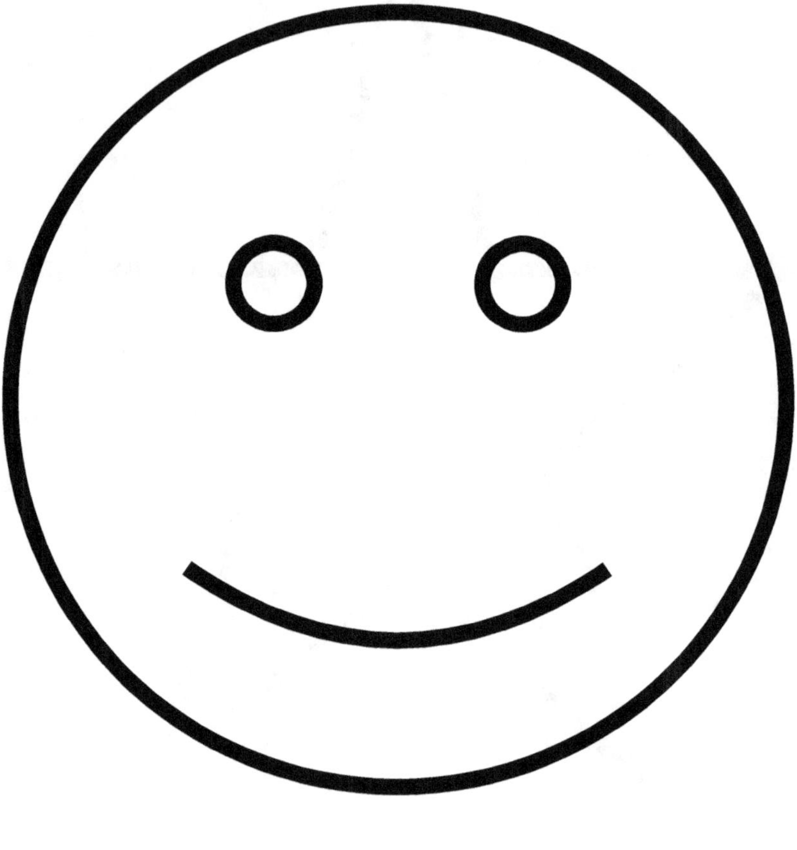

COLOURING BOOK FOR KIDS :1 SHAPES

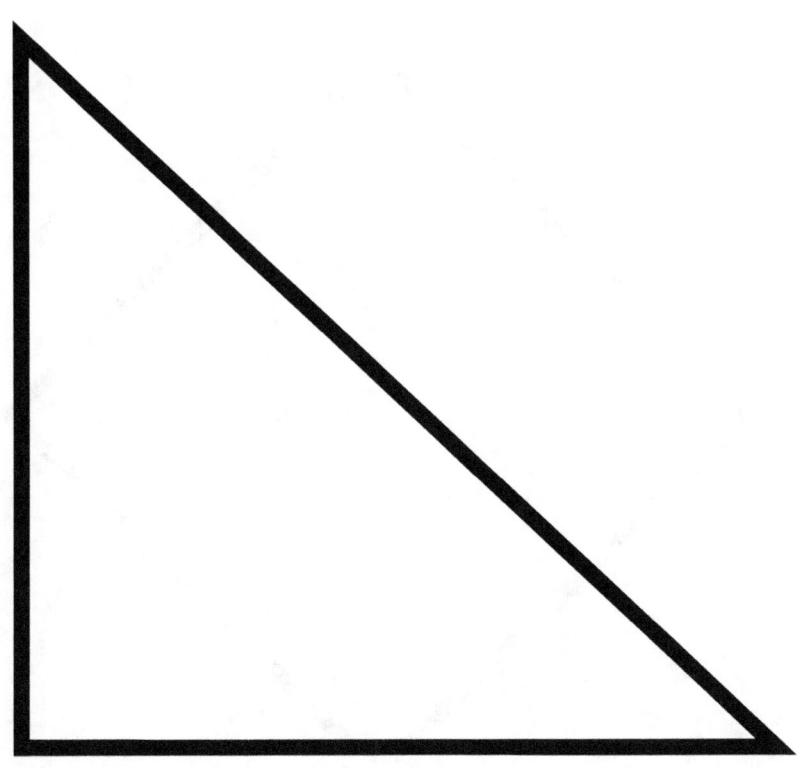

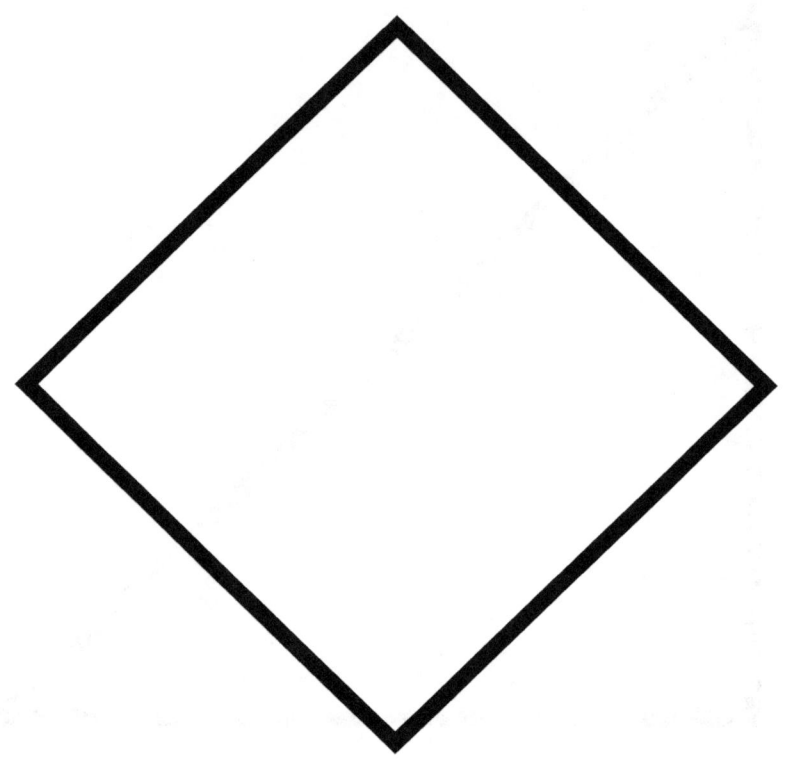

COLOURING BOOK FOR KIDS :1 SHAPES

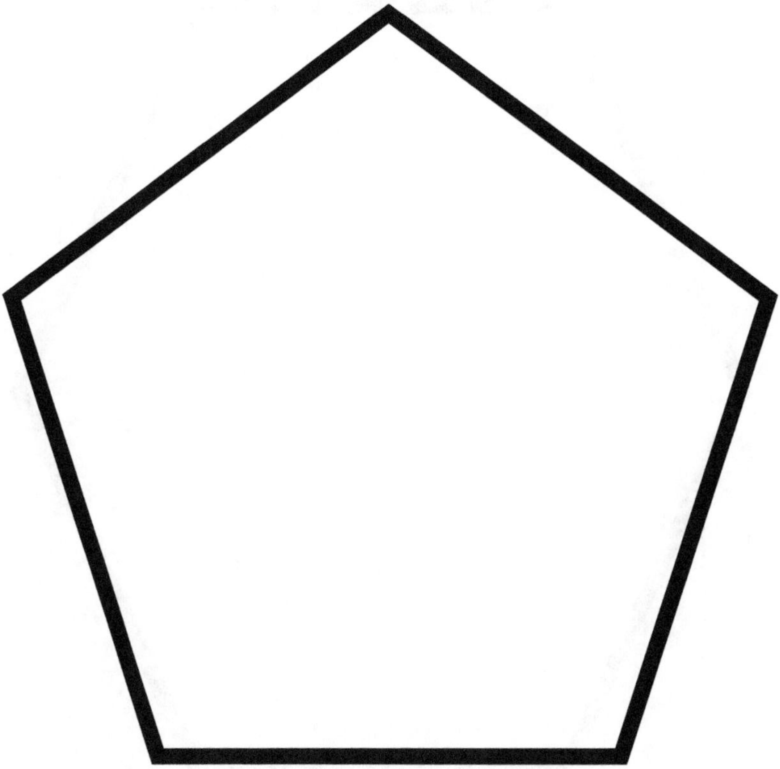

LOURING BOOK FOR KIDS :1 SHAPES

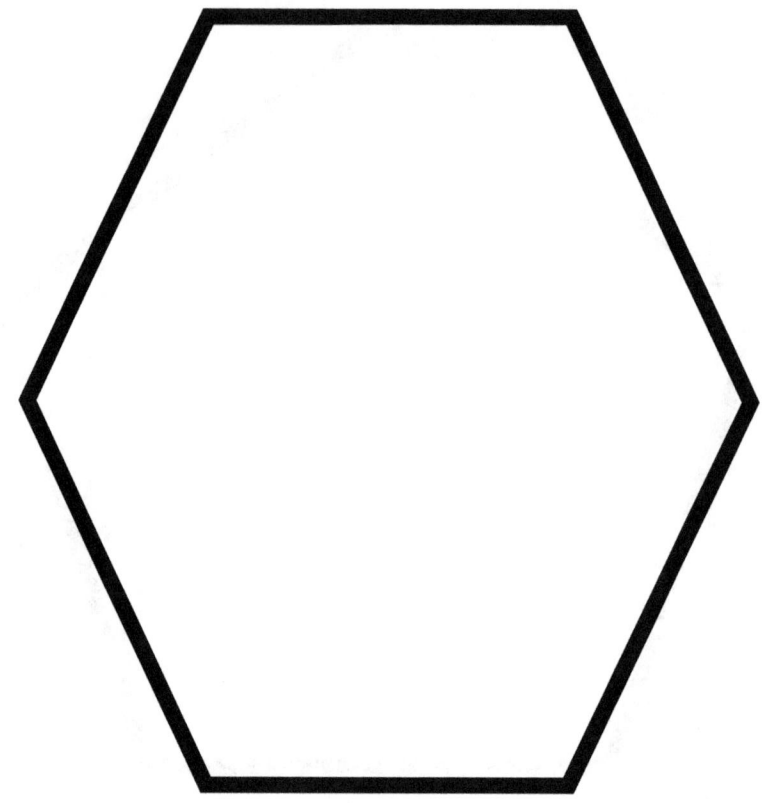

COLOURING BOOK FOR KIDS :1 SHAPES

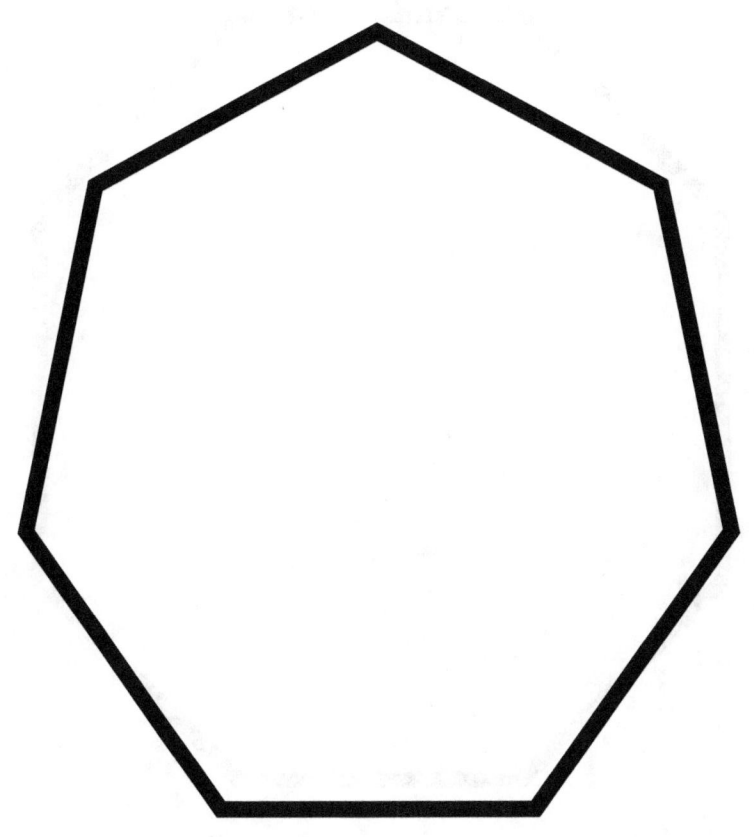

LOURING BOOK FOR KIDS :1 SHAPES

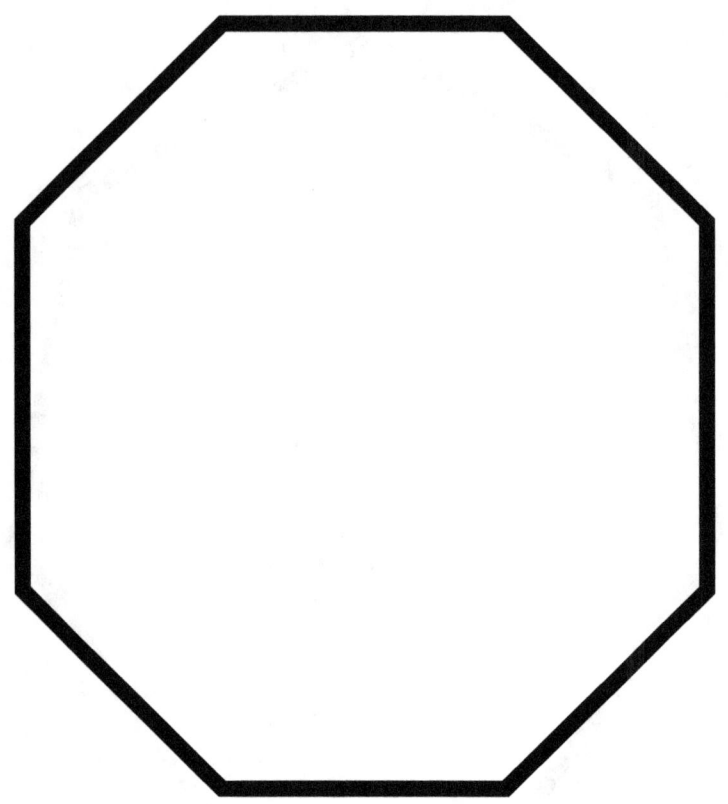

COLOURING BOOK FOR KIDS :1 SHAPES

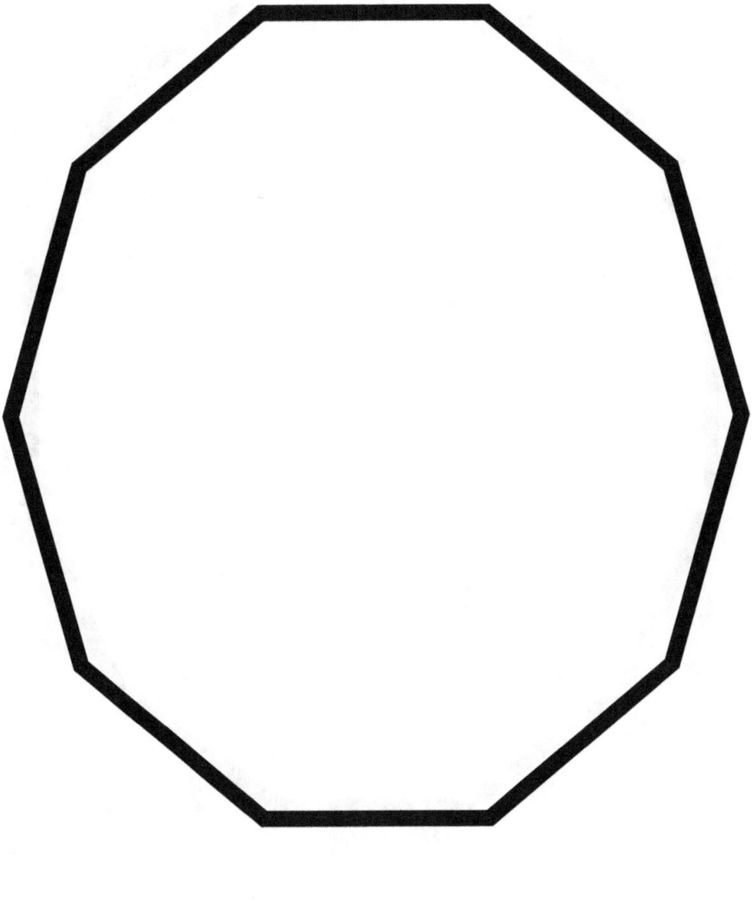

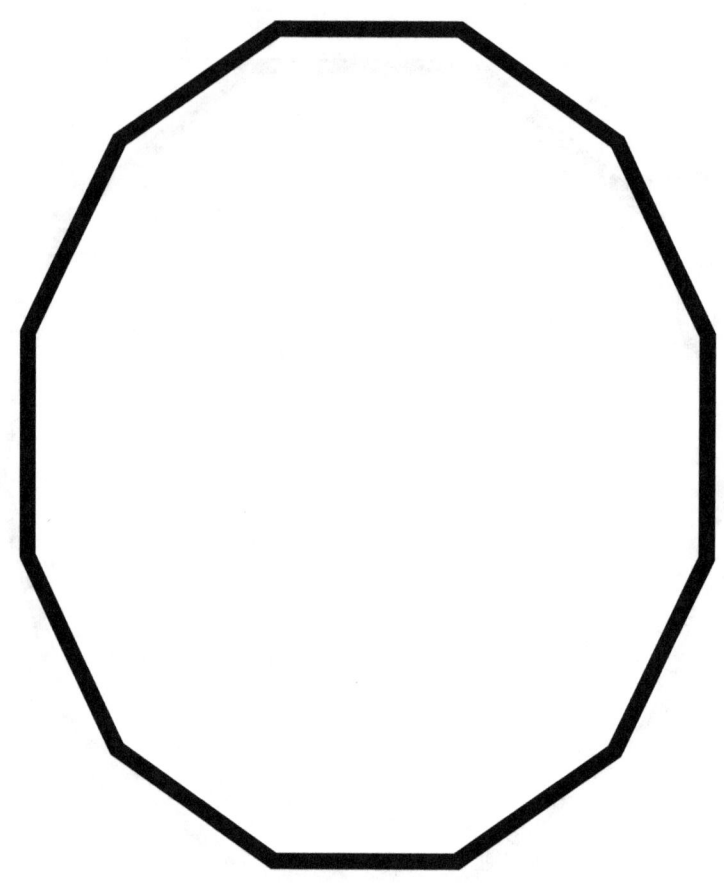

COLOURING BOOK FOR KIDS :1 SHAPES

LOURING BOOK FOR KIDS :1 SHAPES

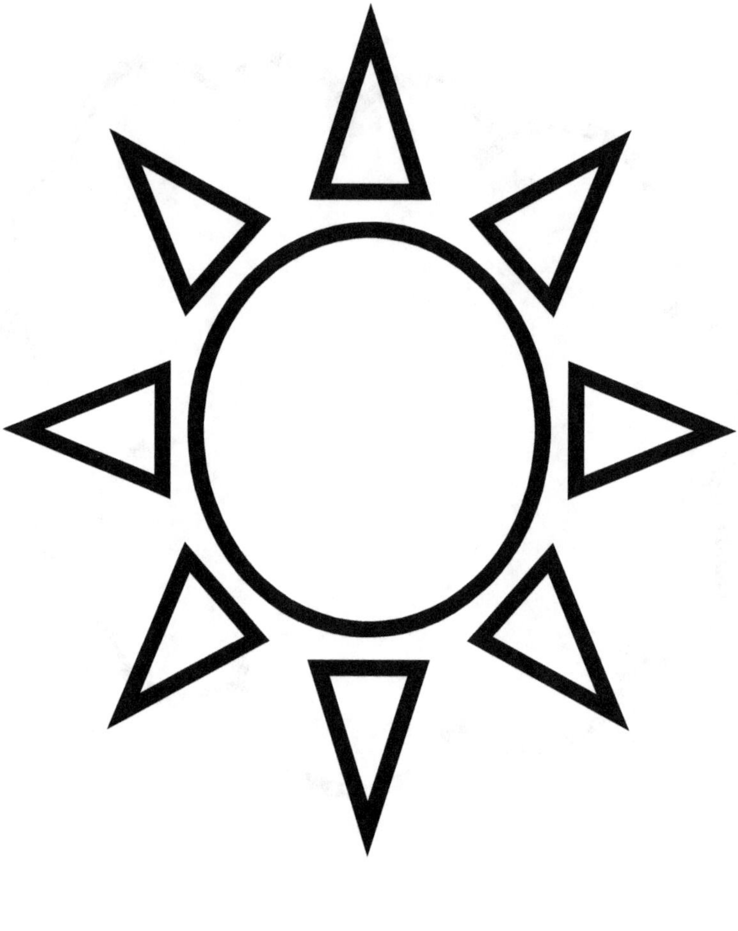

COLOURING BOOK FOR KIDS :1 SHAPES

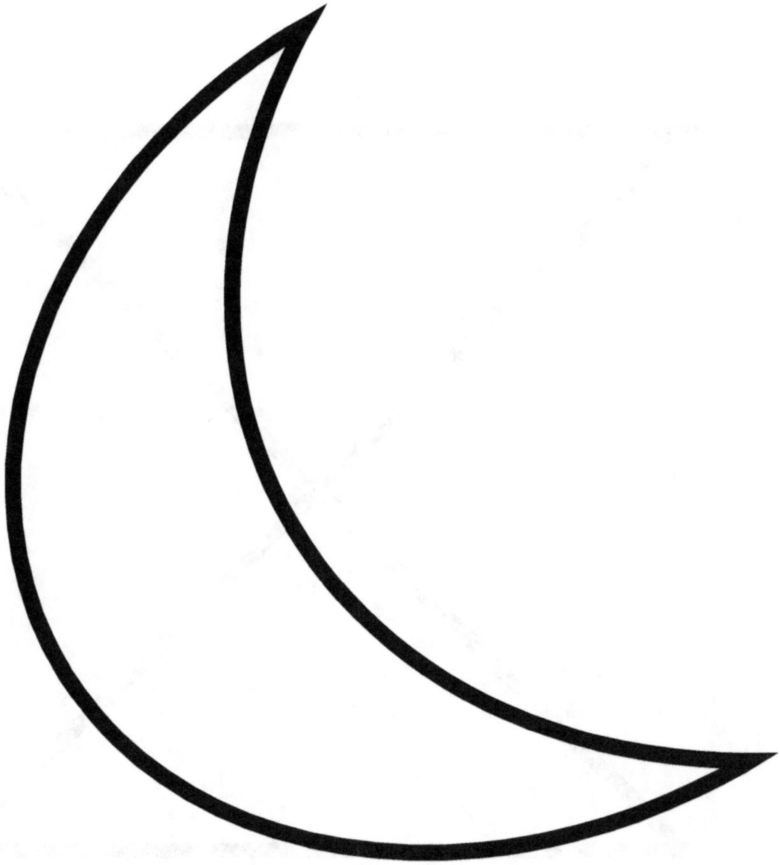

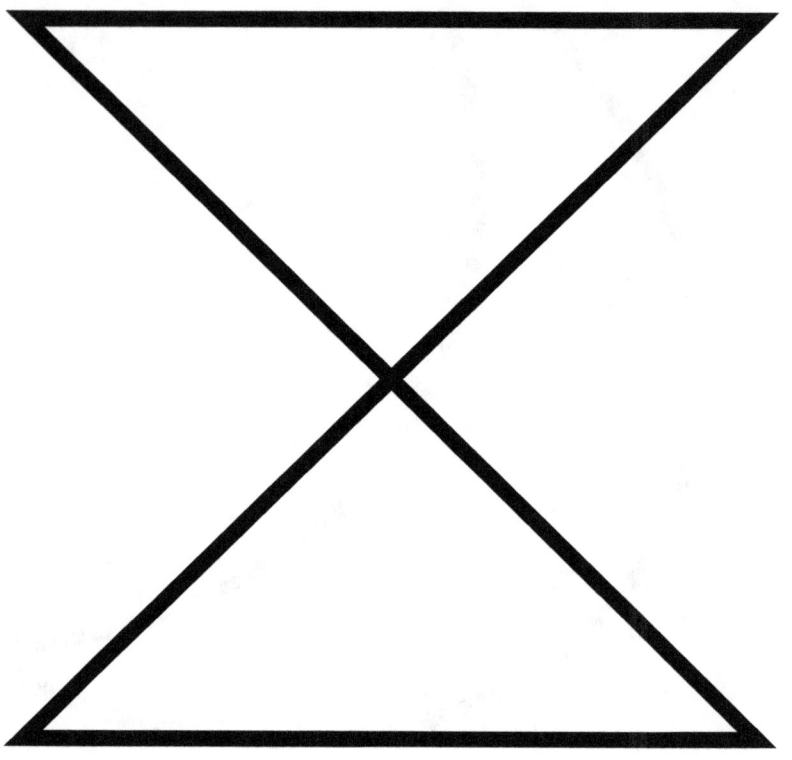

COLOURING BOOK FOR KIDS :1 SHAPES

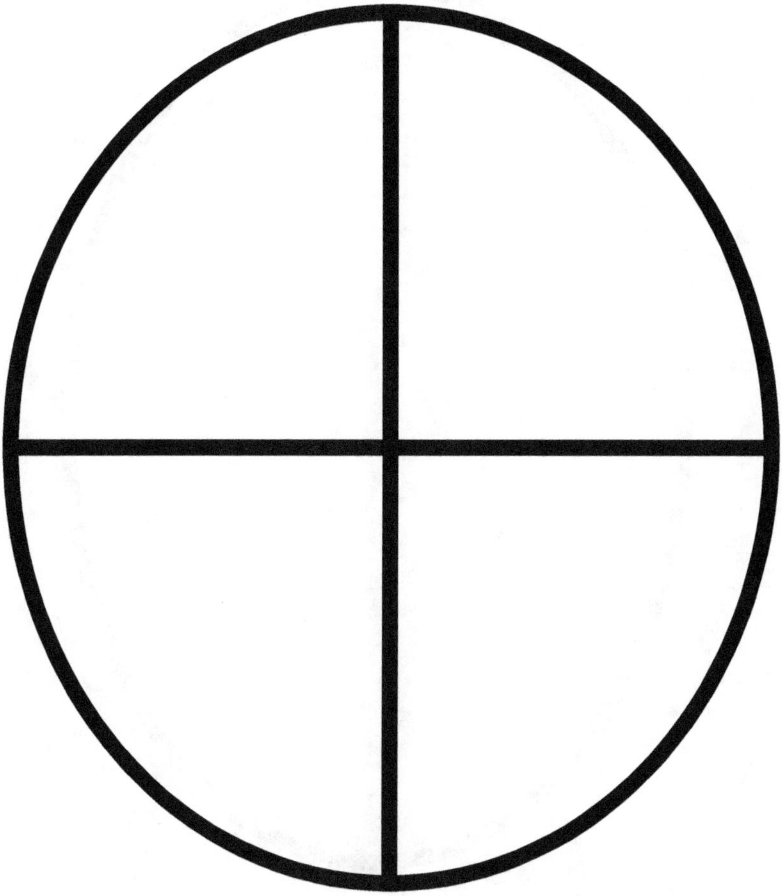

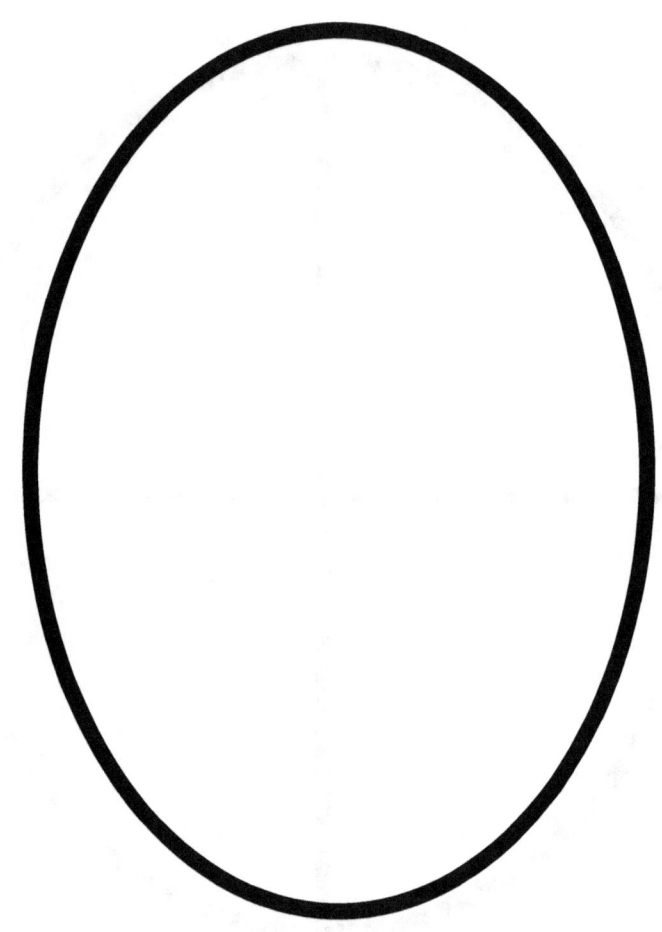

COLOURING BOOK FOR KIDS :1 SHAPES

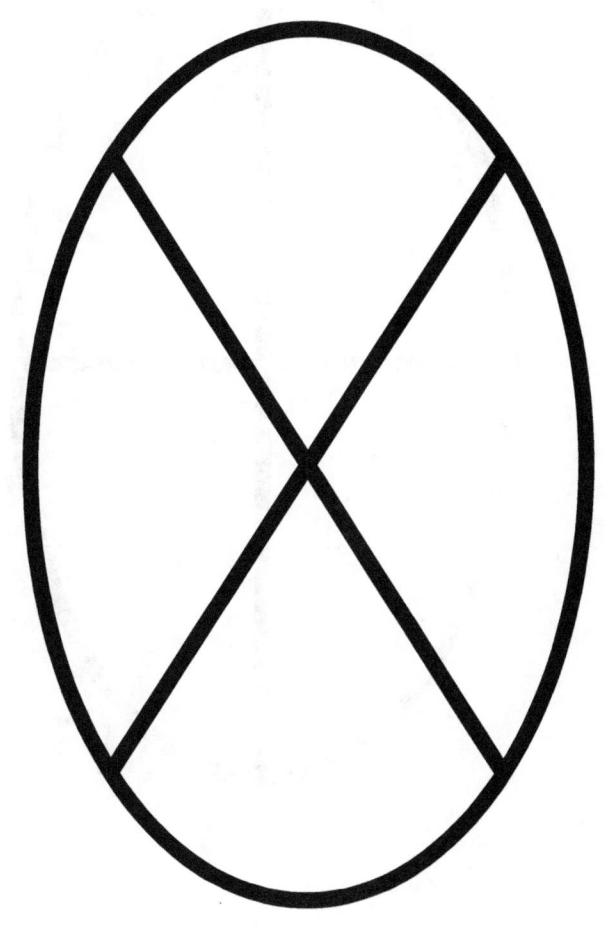

LOURING BOOK FOR KIDS :1 SHAPES

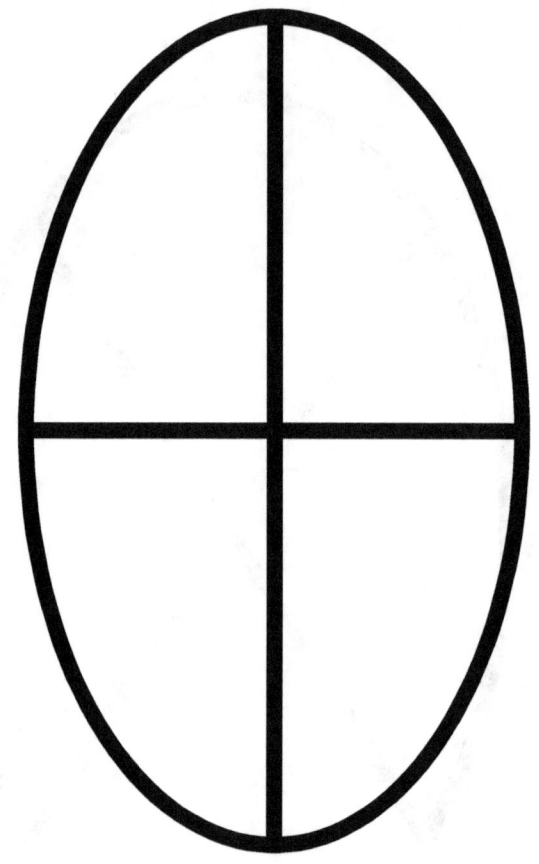

COLOURING BOOK FOR KIDS :1 SHAPES

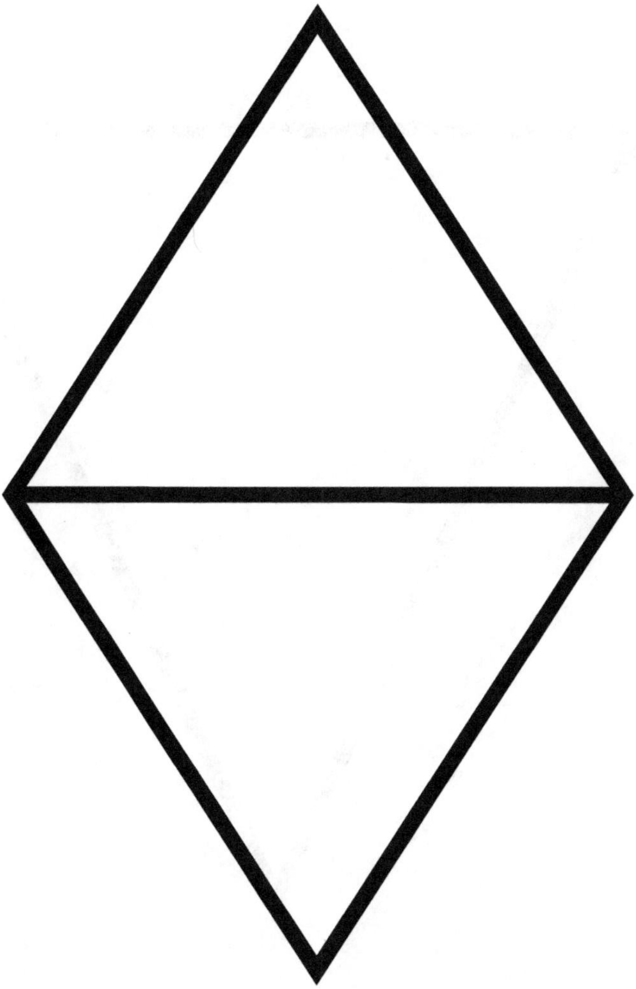

LOURING BOOK FOR KIDS :1 SHAPES

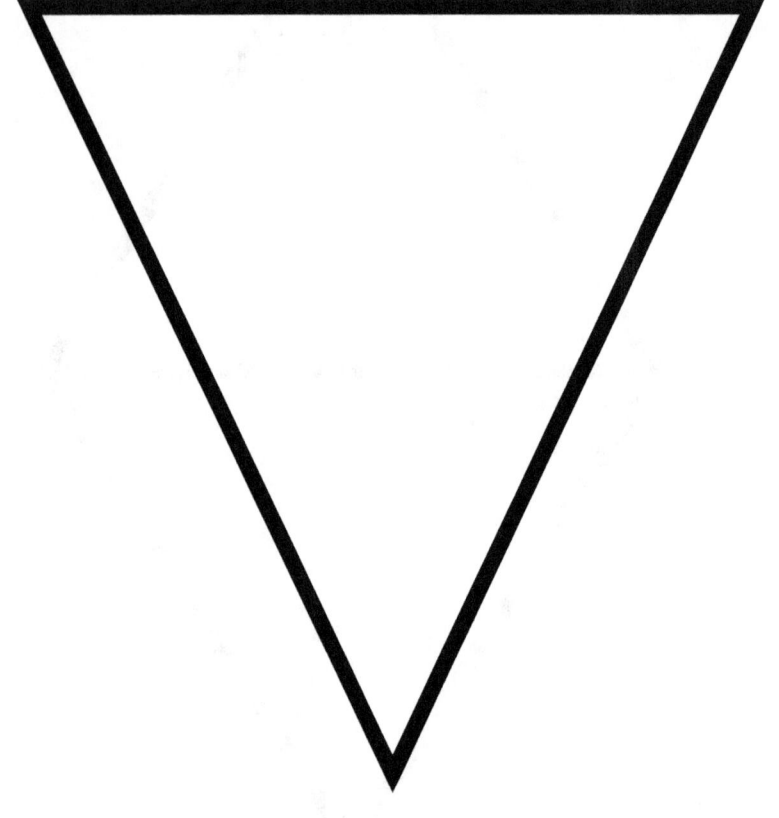

COLOURING BOOK FOR KIDS :1 SHAPES

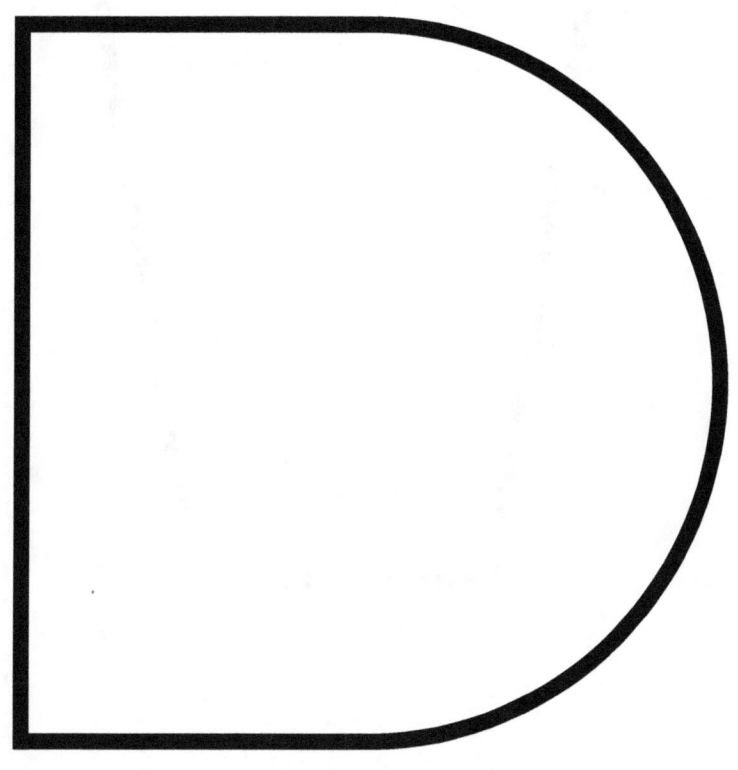

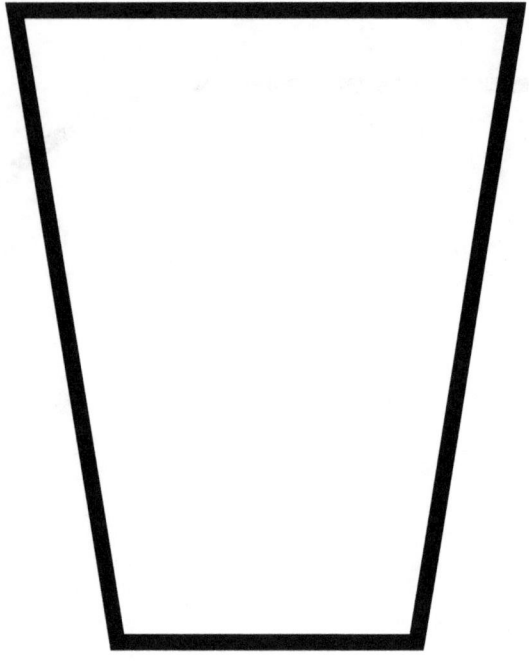

COLOURING BOOK FOR KIDS :1 SHAPES

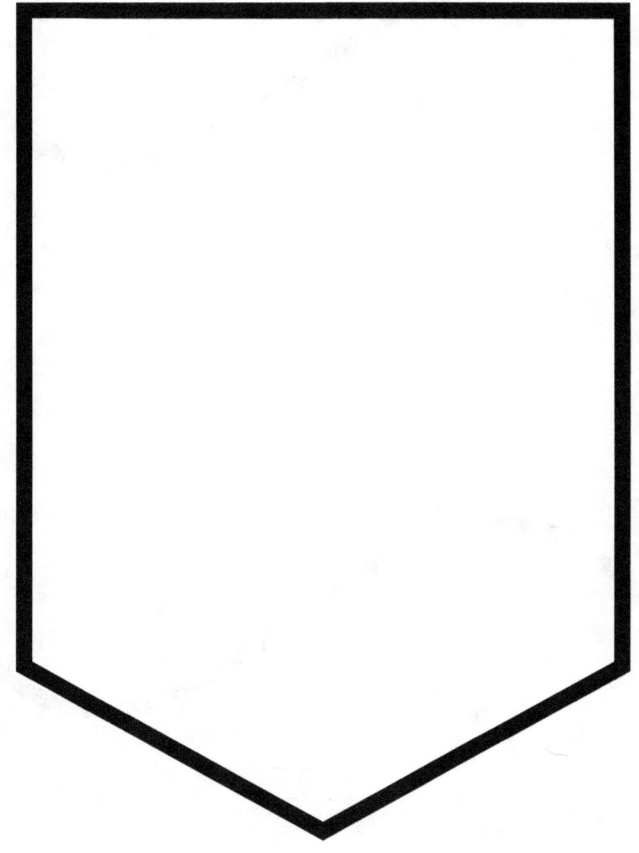

LOURING BOOK FOR KIDS :1 SHAPES

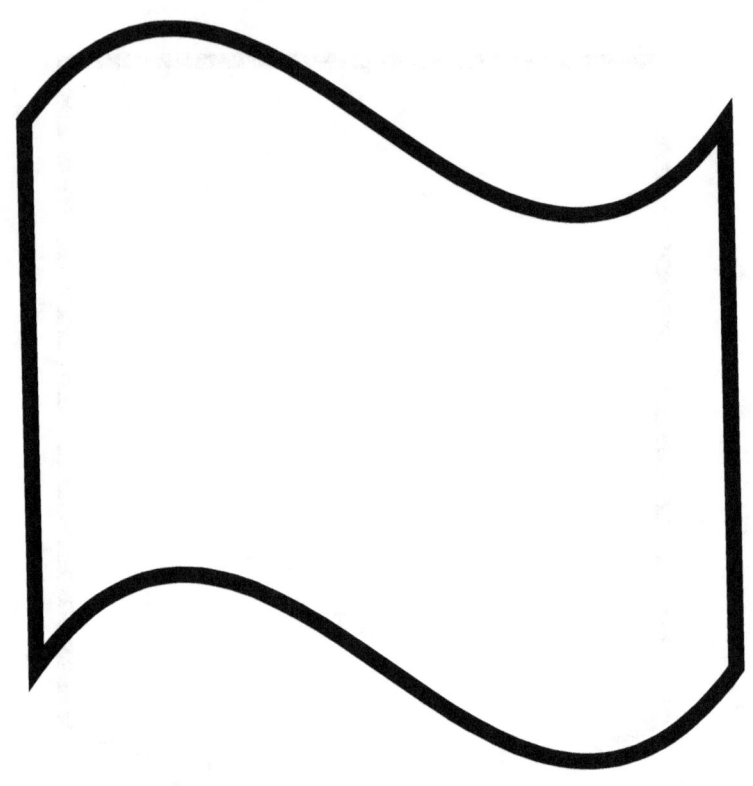

COLOURING BOOK FOR KIDS :1 SHAPES

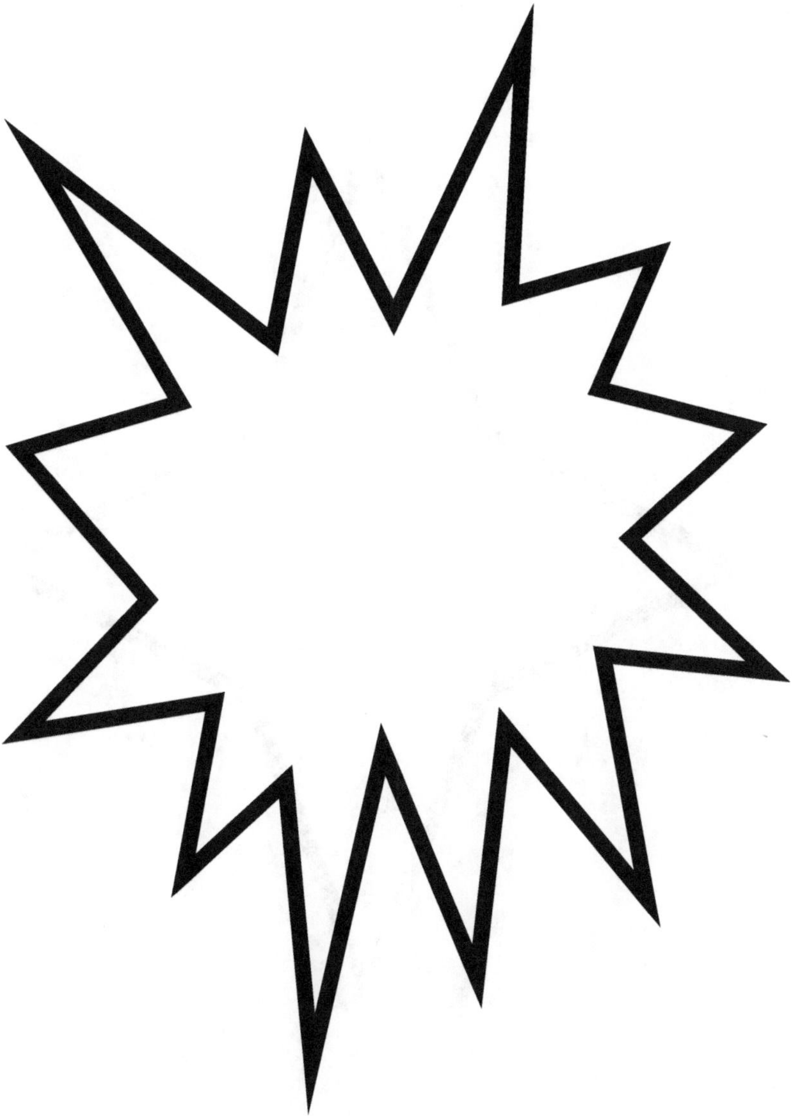

LOURING BOOK FOR KIDS :1 SHAPES

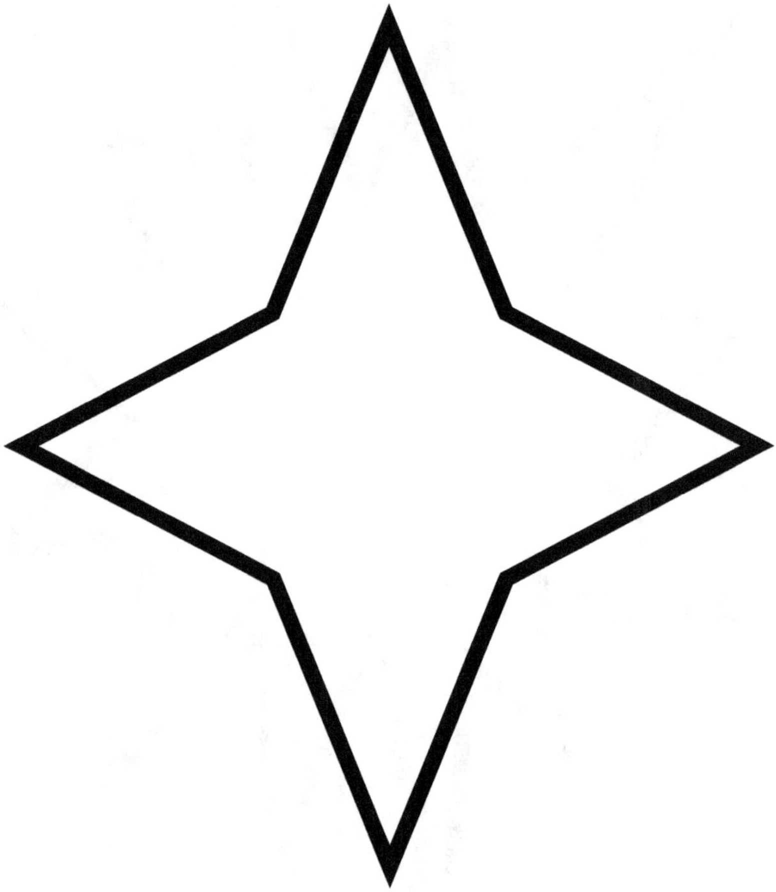

COLOURING BOOK FOR KIDS :1 SHAPES

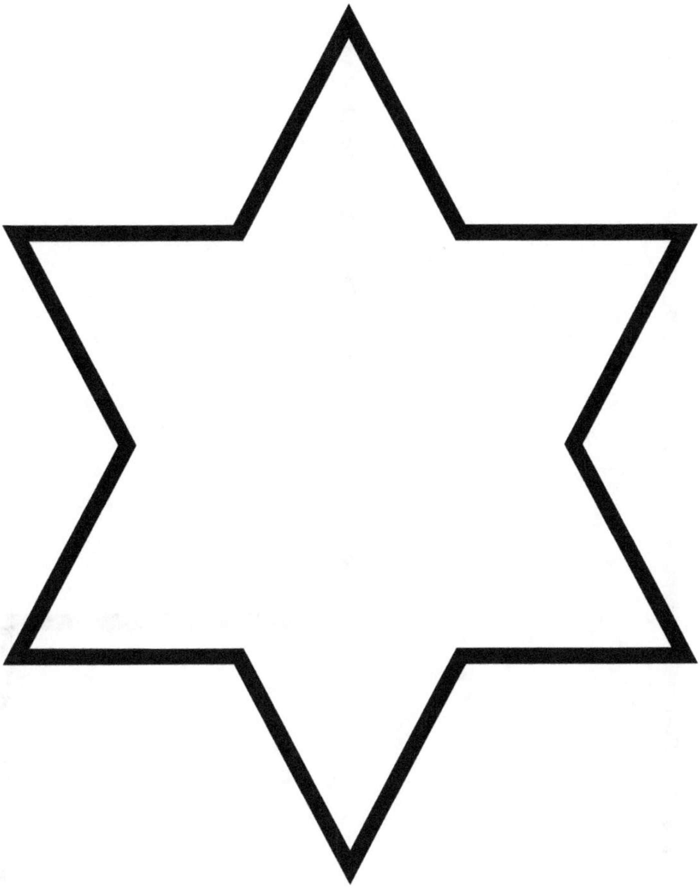

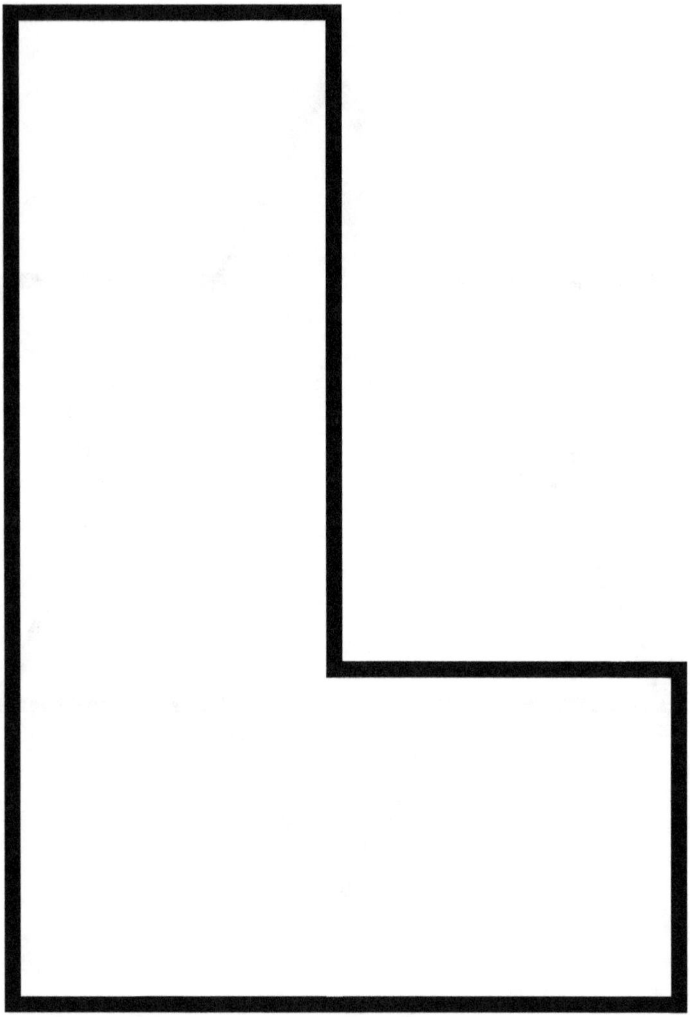

COLOURING BOOK FOR KIDS :1 SHAPES

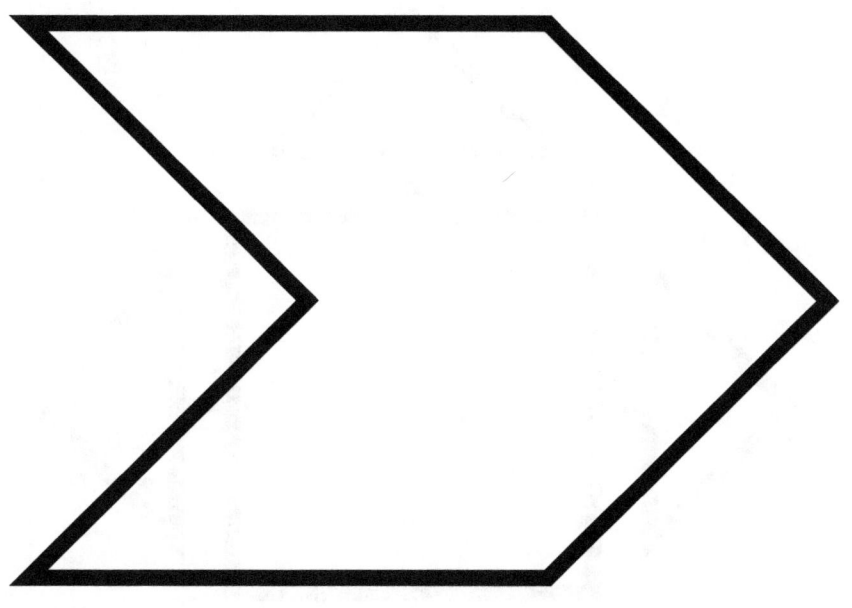

LOURING BOOK FOR KIDS :1 SHAPES

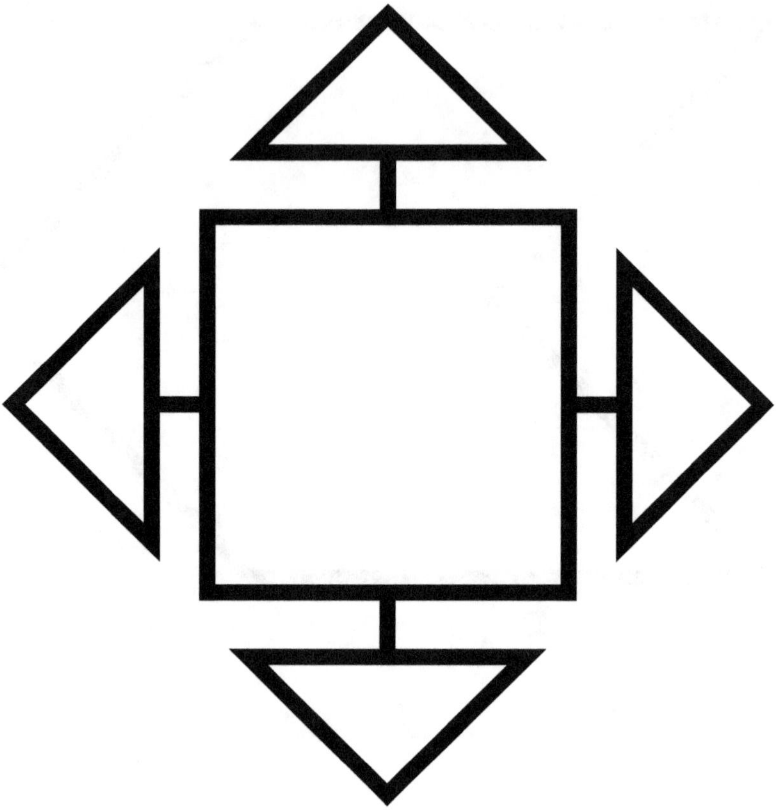

COLOURING BOOK FOR KIDS :1 SHAPES

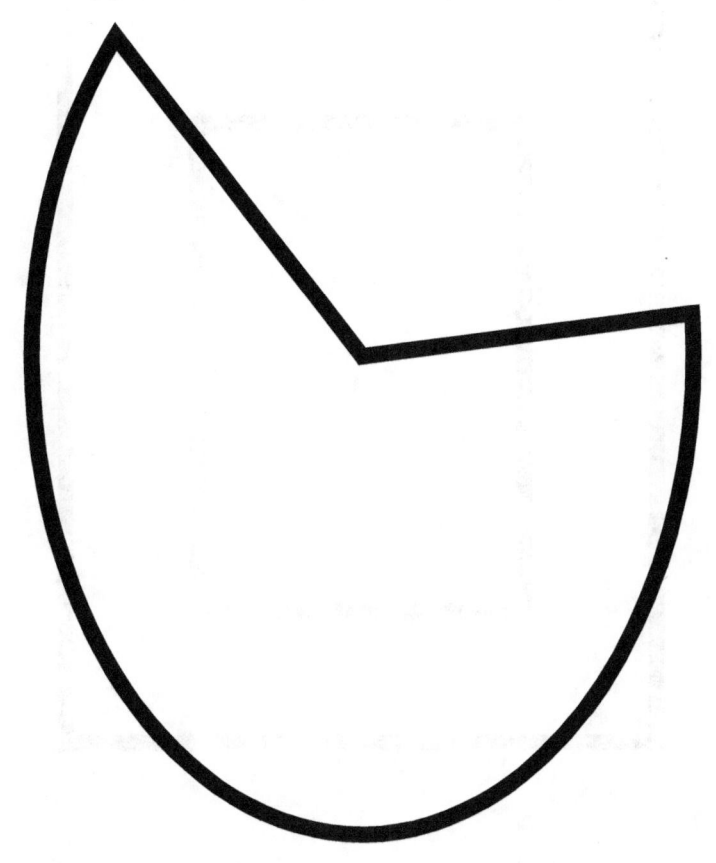

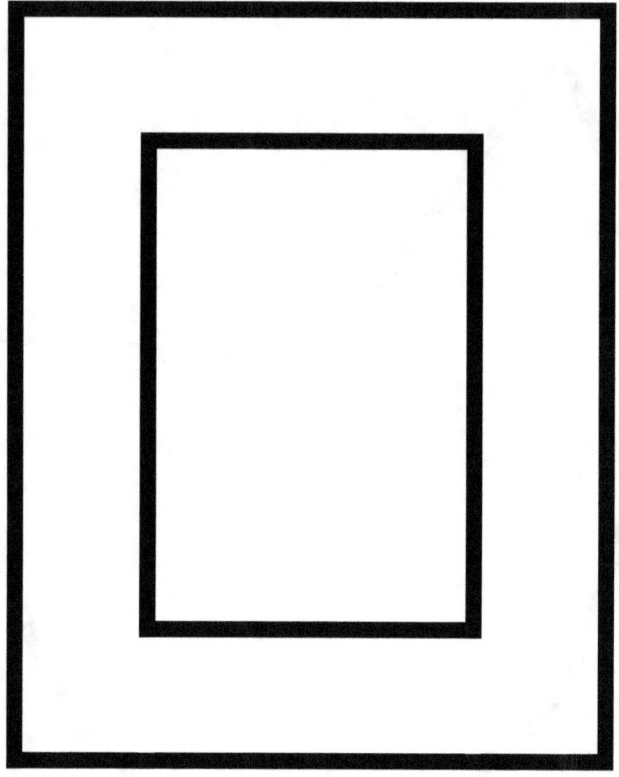

COLOURING BOOK FOR KIDS :1 SHAPES

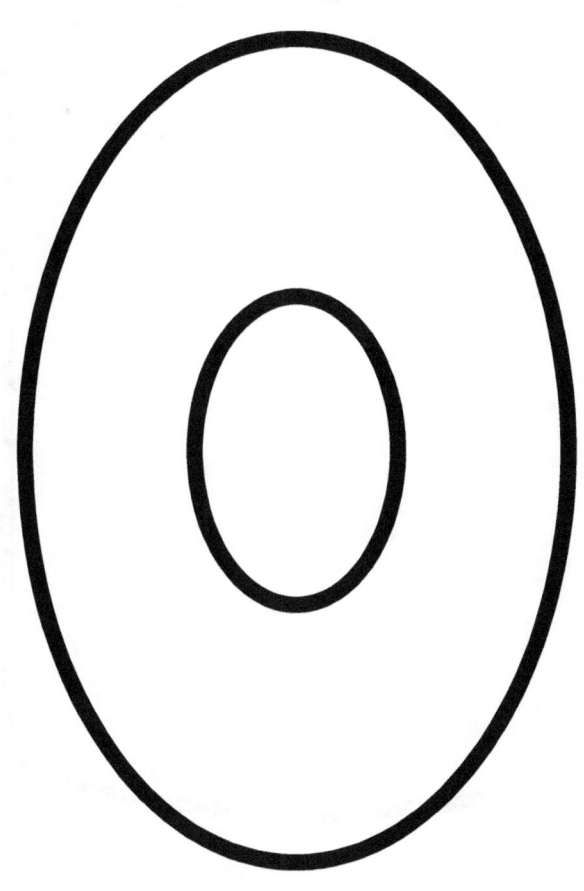

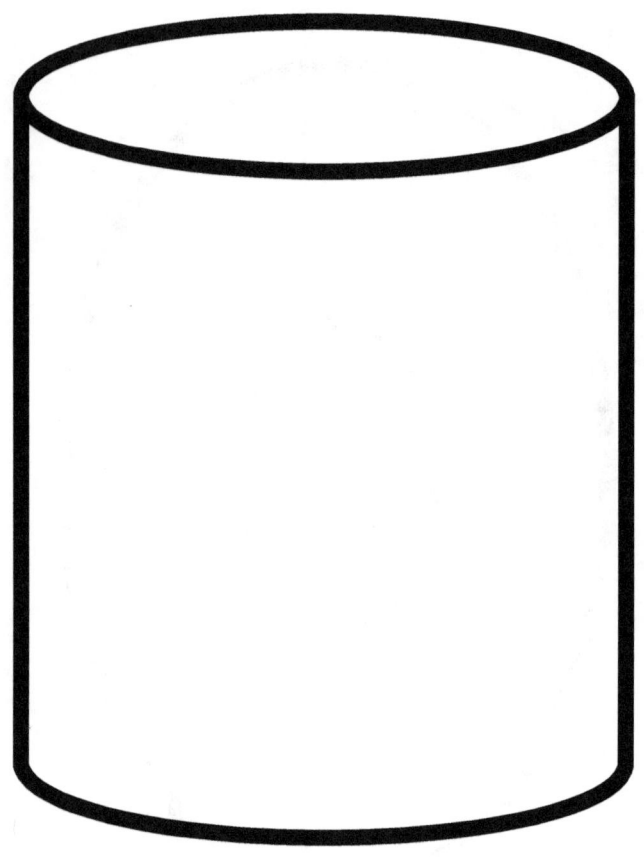

COLOURING BOOK FOR KIDS :1 SHAPES

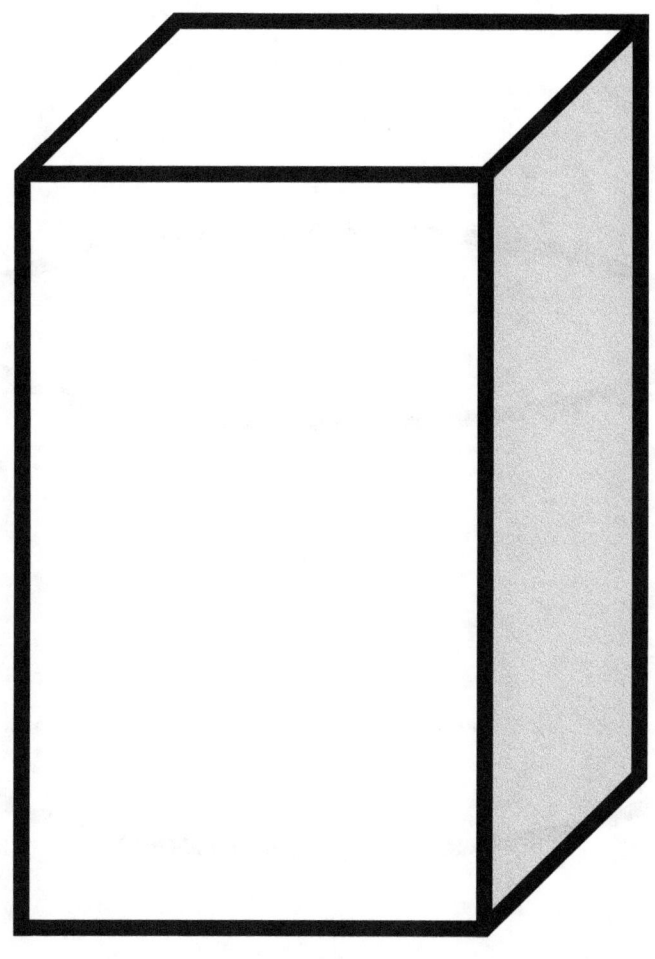

LOURING BOOK FOR KIDS :1 SHAPES

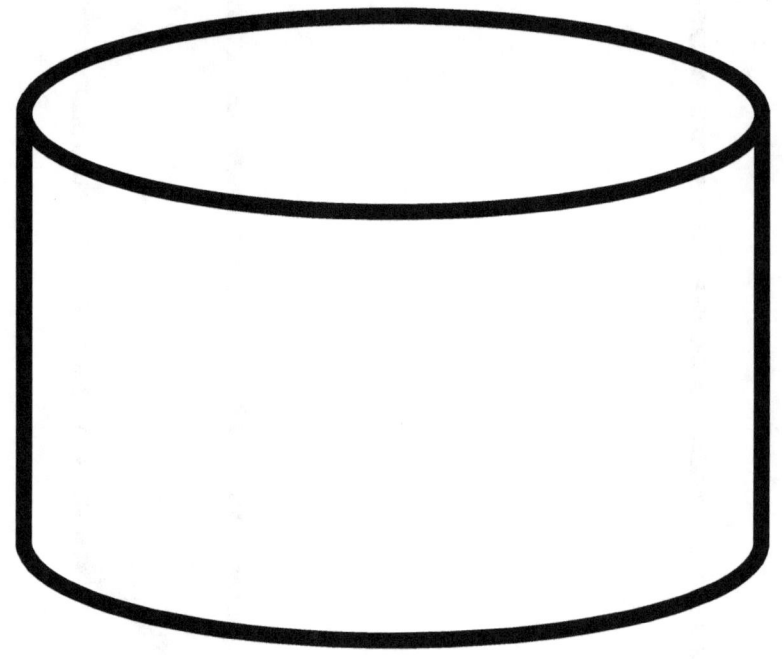

COLOURING BOOK FOR KIDS :1 SHAPES

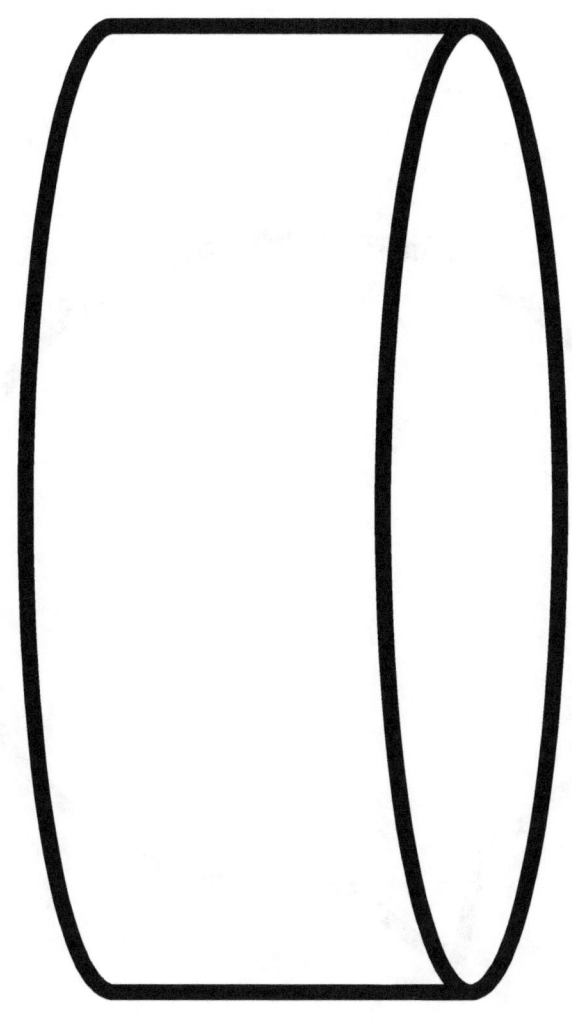

COLOURING BOOK FOR KIDS :1 SHAPES

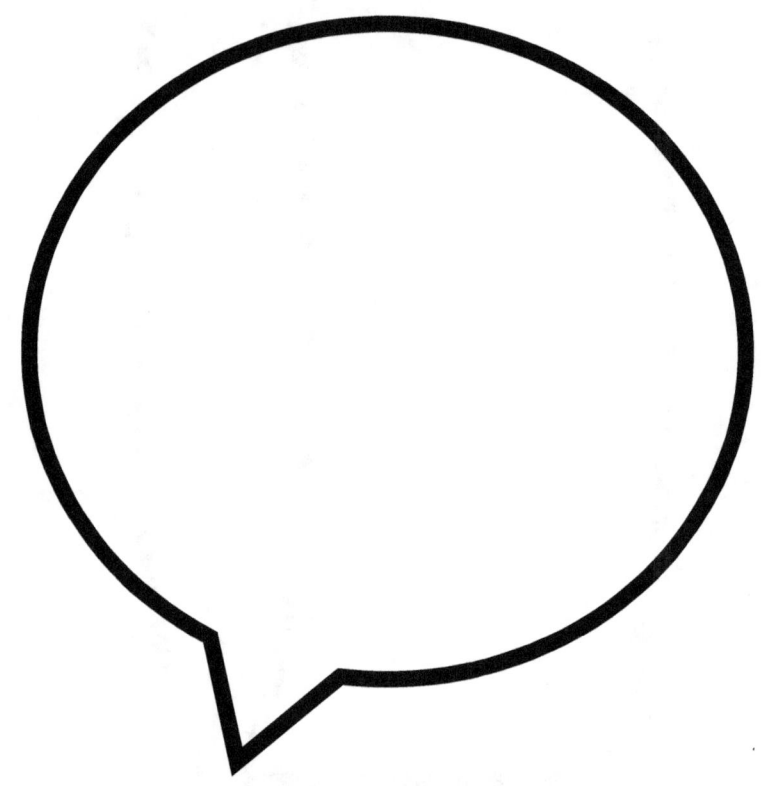

COLOURING BOOK FOR KIDS :1 SHAPES

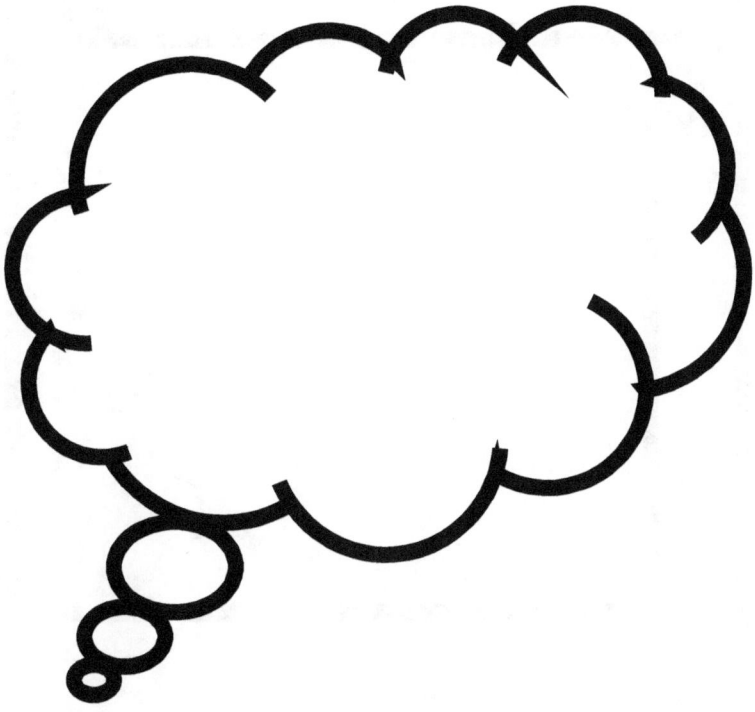

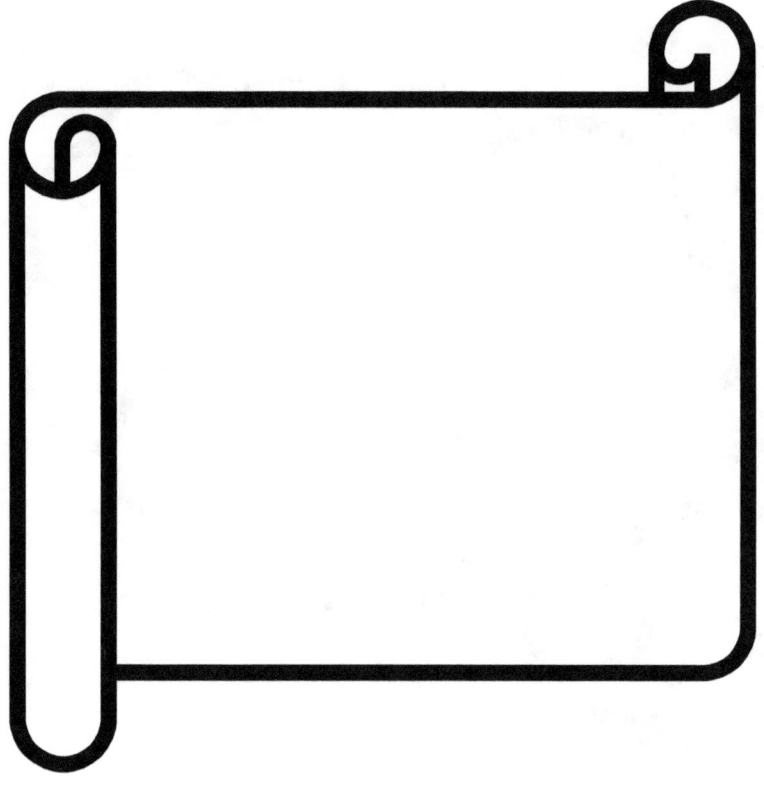

COLOURING BOOK FOR KIDS :1 SHAPES

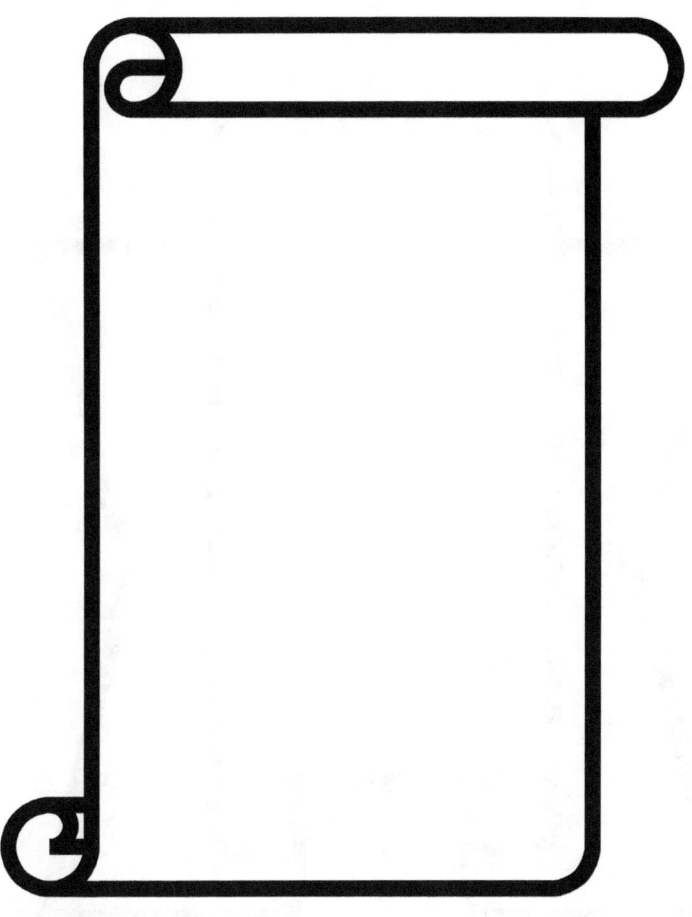

OURING BOOK FOR KIDS :1 SHAPES

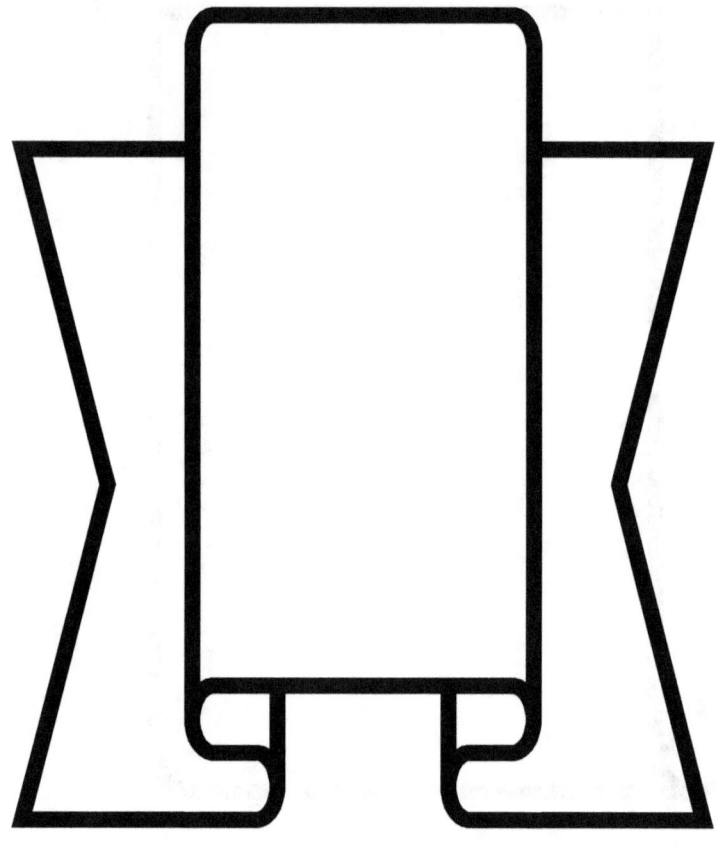

COLOURING BOOK FOR KIDS :1 SHAPES

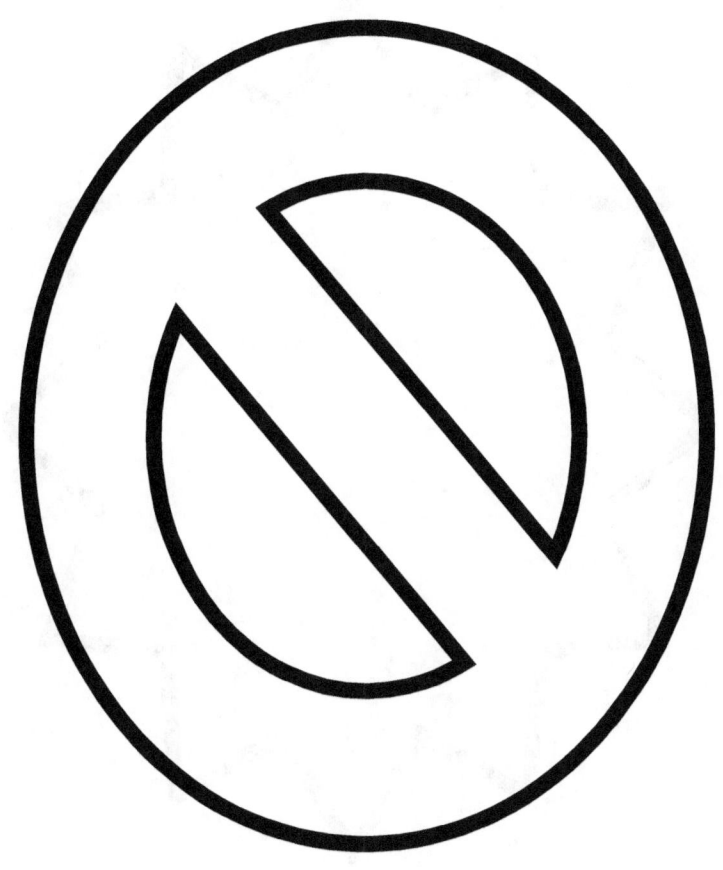

OURING BOOK FOR KIDS :1 SHAPES

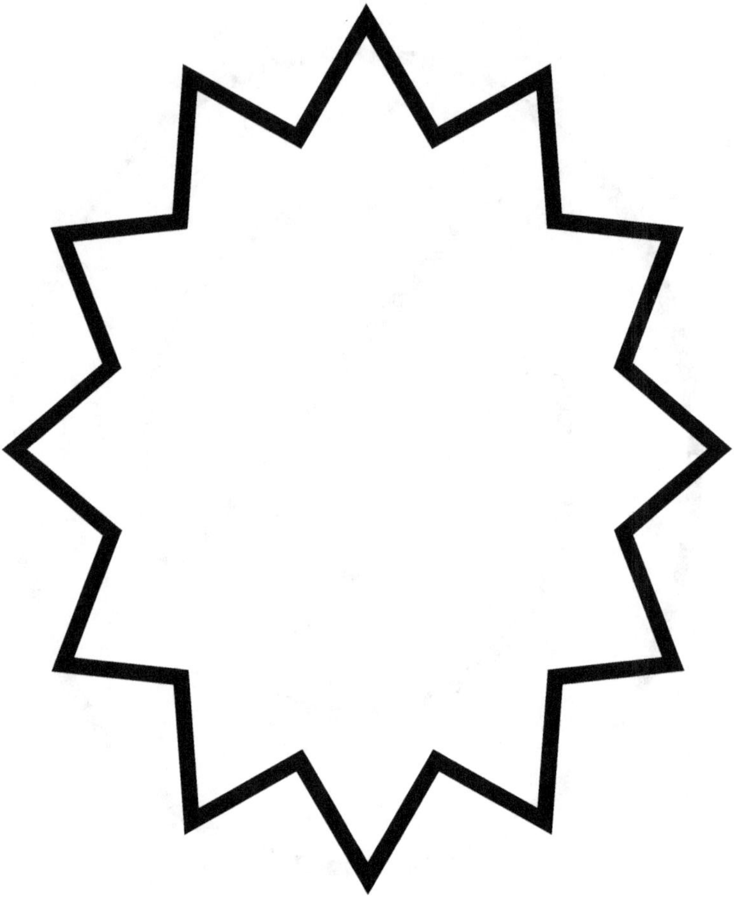

COLOURING BOOK FOR KIDS :1 SHAPES

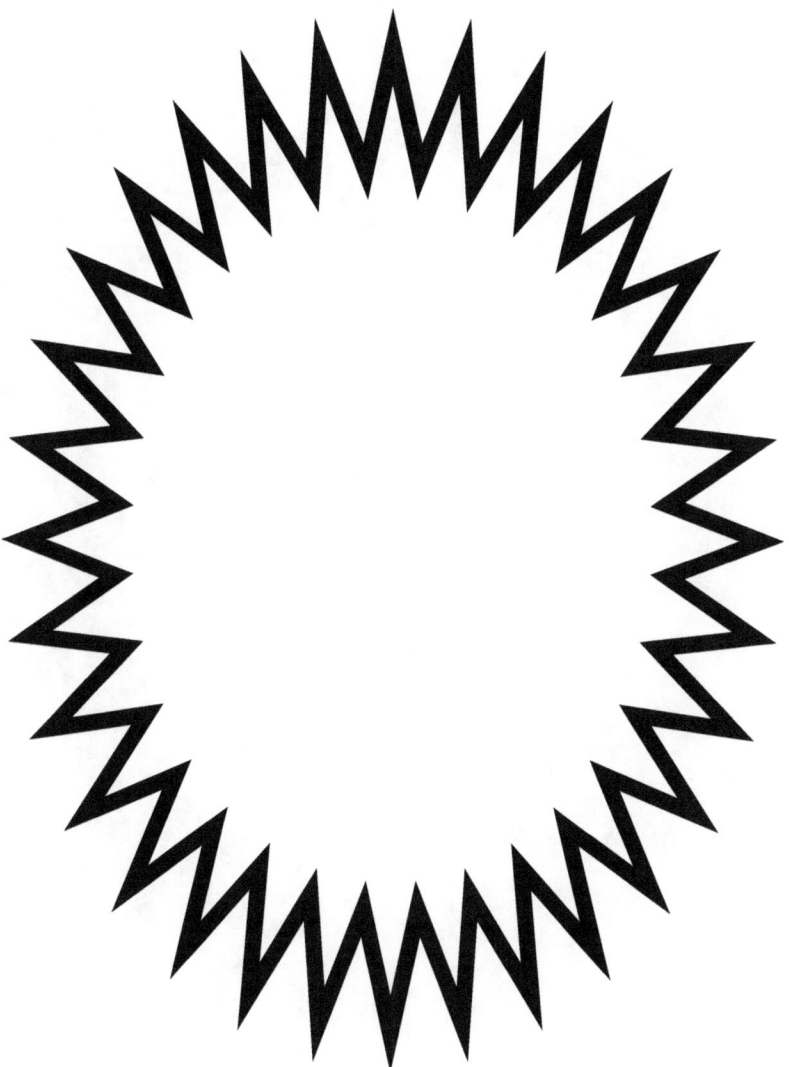

☆ ☆ ☆ ☆ ☆

www.ingramcontent.com/pod-product-compliance
Lightning Source LLC
Chambersburg PA
CBHW072259170526
45158CB00003BA/1111

9 781080 393039